Mastering Breakout Trading: A Step-by-Step Guide Using the Alligator, Gator Oscillator & Efficiency Ratio

Table of Contents

Preface 3

Introduction 4

Understanding Alligator indicator 5

Understanding Gator Indicator 7

Understanding Kaufman's Efficiency Ratio 13

Trade Setup: Buy Conditions 17

Analysis 20

    INDIAN STOCKS 20

Summary 35

Preface

A Realistic Approach to Trading Success

Trading is not a path to instant wealth. Anyone suggesting otherwise is either being deceptive or has made an exceptionally risky trade that worked out by sheer luck.

It is important to understand that trading involves a level of risk that may not be suitable for everyone. The information in this book is provided for educational purposes only. It is strongly recommended that you seek professional financial advice before risking your capital with any trading strategy or system.

This book is designed for traders who are eager to deepen their understanding of technical analysis, particularly in relation to positional trading strategies.

Even if your trading focus is on shorter time frames, you will still find valuable insights here, as the principles and strategies discussed can be effectively applied across all time horizons.

No matter your current level of experience, I am confident that by the end of this book, you will have gained new skills and sharpened your abilities, becoming a more efficient, and most importantly, a more profitable trader.

Introduction

Hello and thank you for purchasing *Mastering Breakout Trading: A Step-by-Step Guide Using the Alligator, Gator Oscillator & Efficiency Ratio.*

In this book, I present a unique trading strategy that is relatively new to the trading profession. You will find a complete trading system with clear, precise entry and exit rules, designed to give you an edge in your trading journey.

This book is primarily tailored for Swing Traders focused on Price Action trading. I introduce you to key strategies and techniques that form a comprehensive system for identifying optimal trade entries, equipping you with the knowledge and tools necessary to succeed in trading.

Whether you are a beginner in the stock market or a seasoned professional, this book will provide valuable insights. The strategies discussed can be applied to any actively traded asset in liquid markets such as Equities, Forex, Commodities, Cryptocurrencies, Bonds, and more.

I hope you find this book both engaging and useful. If you have enjoyed it, please consider recommending it to others and leaving a review on Amazon.

Understanding Alligator indicator

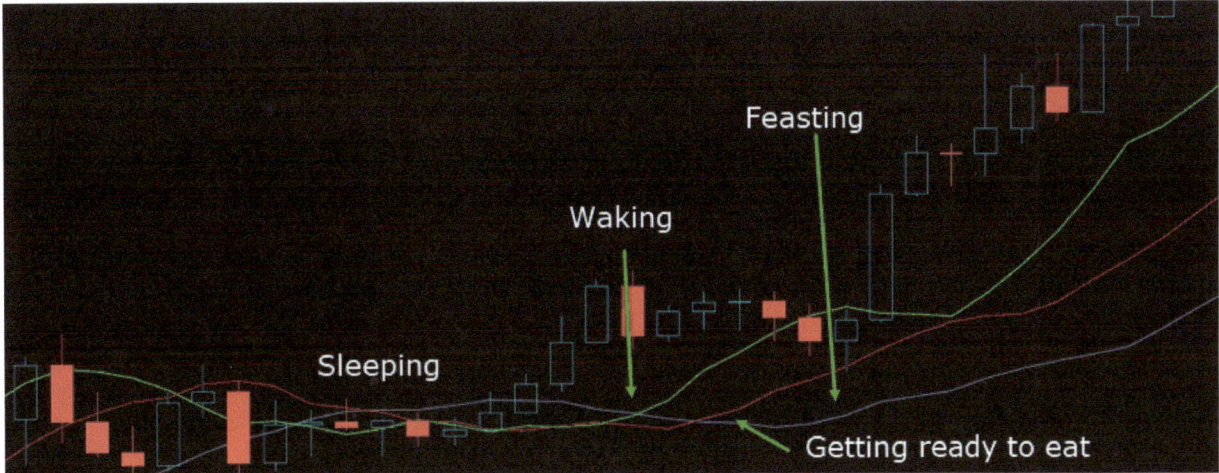

Stages of the Alligator Indicator

The developer of the Alligator indicator was a legendary trader Bill William. According to his belief, traders collect most of their profits during strongly trending periods. In keeping with these lines of thinking, the Alligator indicator was made of three moving averages. Each of the moving averages smoothed over different time-frames, known as 'balance lines'.

In brief, the three lines of the alligator indicator are known as the jaw, teeth and lips. By observing those lines traders can determine trading and breakout strategies. Here, lips, teeth, and jaw of the alligator show the interaction of different time periods.

Alligator indicator trading strategy uses three components, the 13-day simple moving average (SMA), 8-day simple moving average and a 5-day simple moving average. The 13-day SMA is known as alligator jaw and is indicated by the blue line, 8-day SMA is teeth and colored red and the 5-day SMA is known as lip and has a green colored line. These lines help us to identify when there is no trend in the market. It also helps us in understanding when the trend is forming and in which direction.

When these lines are close together, it denotes no trend. When the 3 lines are intertwined, we do not have a trend. This is generally a time of low volatility and most traders may want to find another instrument to trade

On the other hand, when these balance lines are far from each other it denotes a strong trend in the market. The lips of the Alligator, the green line, is the fastest moving average and will be the first one a trader will want to monitor. You want to see the green line cross both of the slower moving averages. This is a sign that the Alligator is waking up.

The Alligator indicator is best to use on the daily time frame. This indicator is particularly good in trend trading.

Conclusion

- The most important part of the Bill Williams Alligator is when the 3 lines are mixed together. This is when the Alligator is considered to be sleeping and no trading signals are present.
- You should keep these instruments on your radar especially if price action is hinting at an increase in momentum. The best time to get on board a trend move is just before it happens.

Understanding Gator Indicator

- The Gator Oscillator was developed by Bill Williams as an adjunct tool to the Alligator Indicator. This Oscillator is an auxiliary oscillator to the mighty Alligator indicator. It is most useful in markets that display strong directional action

- The Gator Oscillator is a supplement to the Williams Alligator and is used alongside with it showing the absolute degree of convergence/divergence of the Alligator's three SMAs pointing at the Alligator's periods of slumber and awakeness (i.e. trending and non-trending market phases). It also identifies trend changes in securities prices. The main difference between the Gator Oscillator and the Alligator Indicator is that the former uses a histogram while the later uses moving averages.

- Three areas are highlighted in the Oscillator: the jaws, the teeth, and the lips. In the alligator indicator chart, the alligator is said to be up and ready to fill up when all three rows representing these three areas are in the correct order which is jaws at the bottom (blue line), teeth at the middle (red line), and lips on top (green line). In a Gator Oscillator, these values are represented in a histogram by colored bars. An alligator that fills up after eating is indicated by a red bar and a green bar. Both these charts are useful in triggering buy or sell orders from traders depending on what their trading strategy is.

- The different stages of the oscillator in 'Alligator' with two symmetrical bars. One is above the 0 line and another is below the 0 line. Sometimes both bars are green, sometimes both are red and sometimes they are of both colors. A green bar indicates the trend is stronger than the previous price action. While the red bar indicates that the trend is weaker than the previous price action.

How to Use Gator Oscillator

- Being an oscillator in the form of two histograms built on either side of the naught line, the Gator Oscillator plots the absolute difference between the Alligator's Jaw and Teeth (blue and red lines) in the positive area and the absolute difference between the Alligator's Teeth and Lips (red and green lines) in the negative area. The histogram's bars are colored green if exceeding the previous bar's volume or red if falling short. The bars of the extreme values are in tune with the strong trend forces.

- The underlying principle of the Gator indicator is that the trend goes through some phases, just like a living creature, an alligator. We distinguish 4 phases:
    1. Gator sleeps - The bars on both sides are red. The sleeping phase is when the trend is exhausted.

    2. Gator awakes - The bars on different sides of the naught line are colored differently. The Awakening is when a new trend is forming.

    3. Gator eats - Green bars on both sides of the naught line. Eating means getting strength.

    4. Gator Sated - Single red bar during the "eating" phase, meaning running out of momentum.

The Gator Oscillator indicator helps to identify these 4 phases in a trend lifecycle. It helps you to enter a trend as it forms and exit before the trend ends

Sleeping: In the Sleep phase, both bars, below and above the middle line, are red.

Figure 1: ITC Ltd. Daily Chart, The sleep phase is when both upper and lower bars are red

Awakening: We know the trend begins to form when one of the bars, which were previously red, becomes green. It may be the one below or above the 0 line. It only matters that one of two is green.

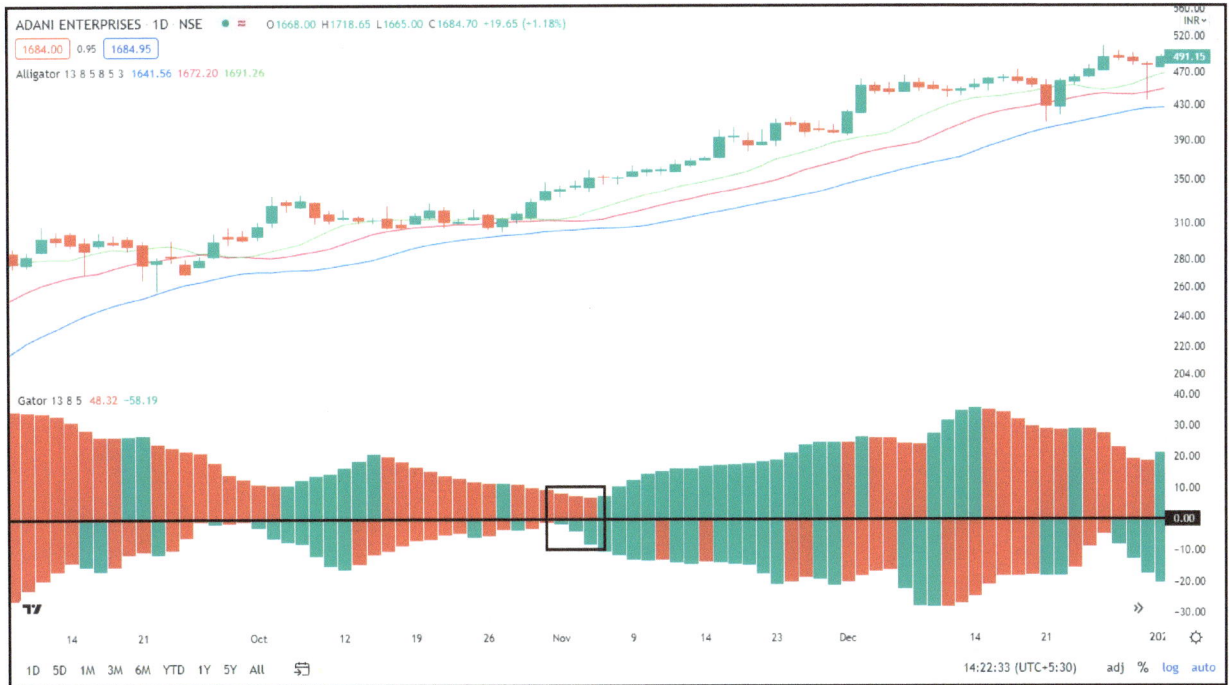

Figure 2: Adani Enterprises Ltd. Daily Chart, Gator awakens after sleeping when a green bar appears.

Eating: The trend is growing which is indicated by two green bars.

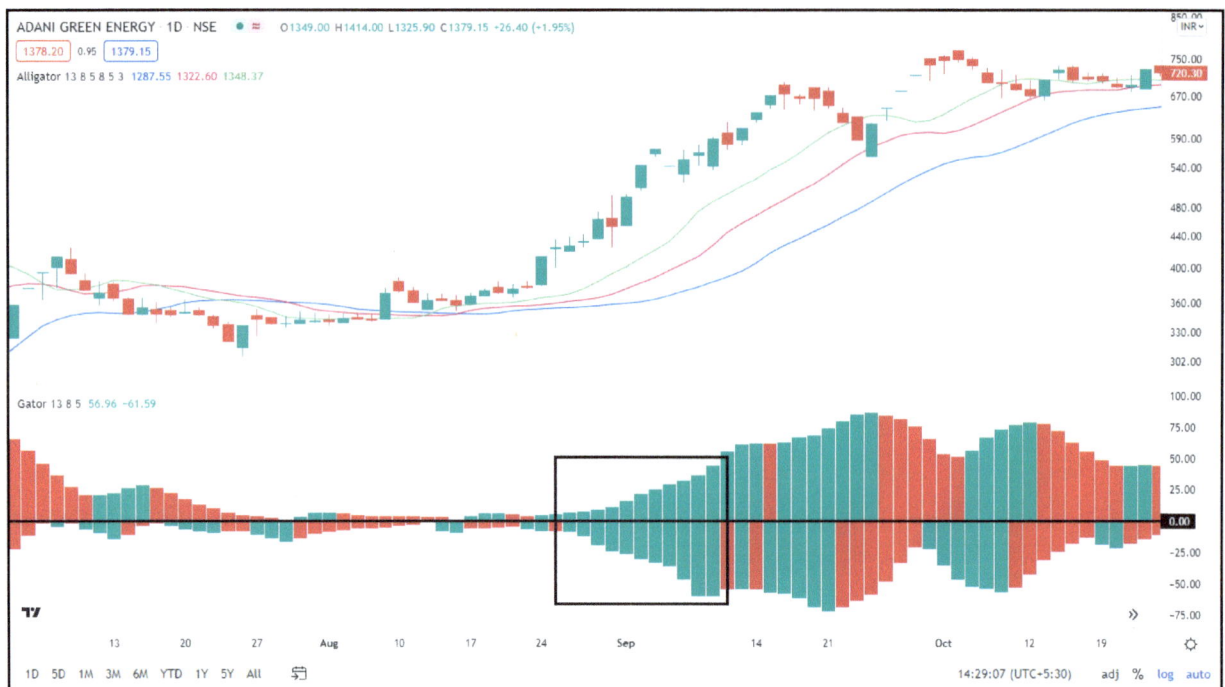

Figure 3: Adani Green Energy Ltd. Daily Chart, The market is trending when both bars are green.

Sated: The animal is full, the trend is coming to an end. On the Gator's histogram, a red bar reappears. Similarly, as in the Awakening phase, it could be a lower or upper bar. What is important is that one of the bar turns red.

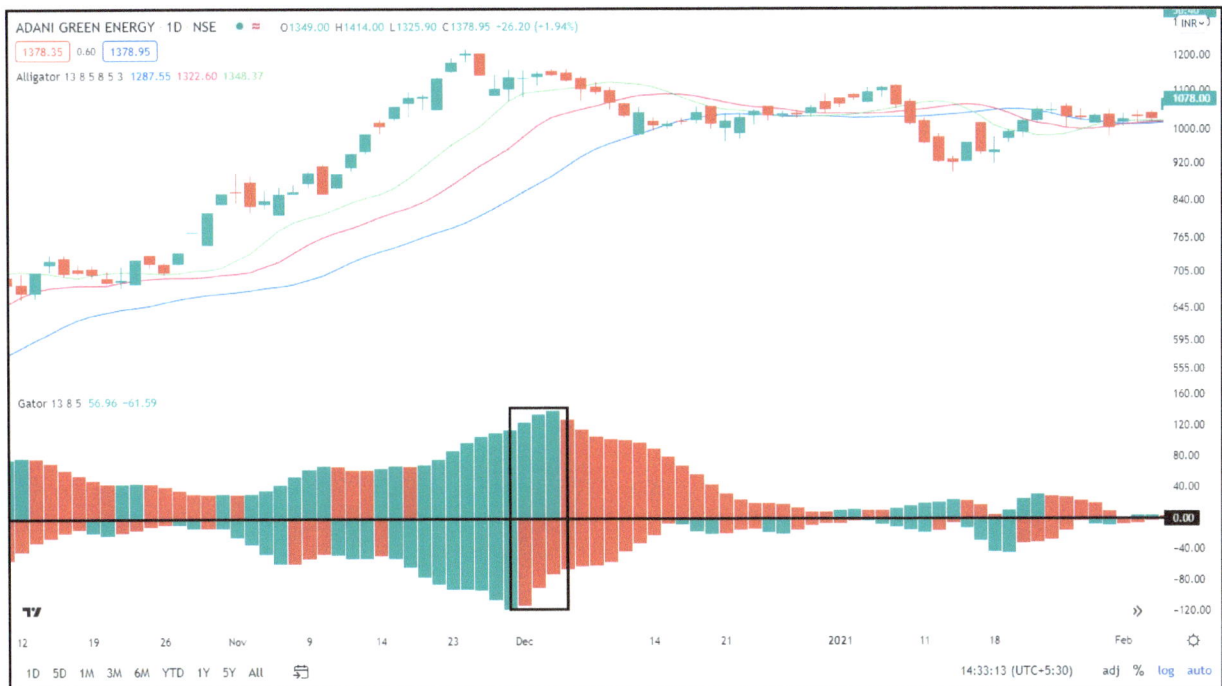

Figure 4: Adani Green Energy Ltd. Daily Chart, A red bar after a series of green bars indicates that the trend may end soon

Gator Oscillator Indicator Calculation

First, calculate the difference between the long-term moving average which is the blue line and the medium-term moving average which is the red line bars above in the 0 (zero). Then calculate the difference between the medium-term moving average which is the red line and short-term moving average which is green line bars below in the 0 (zero). In the Alligator indicator, the Jaw is the blue line, Teeth is the red line and Lips is the green line. But the oscillator consists of only green and red bars. Here each time period is represented by 2 bars, one top of the other.

Upper Gator = Jaw - Teeth

Lower Gator = - (Absolute negative value of (Teeth - Lips))

where:

Upper Gator - is the GATOR value of the line or bar above the centerline.

Lower Gator - is the GATOR value of the line or bar below the centerline.

Jaw - is the longer-period ALLIGATOR value.

Teeth - is the medium-period ALLIGATOR value.

Lips - is the shorter-period ALLIGATOR value.

Conclusion

- The Gator oscillator can be successfully applied in all market conditions however, the best results you will get on medium to longer timeframes.

- The Gator indicator is an oscillator that can be used to identify the changes in the trend. It has a form of histogram with red and green bars. Depending on the colors of the bars, we recognise the Sleeping phase, Awakening, Eating and Sated. Typically, traders enter the position during the Awakening phase, keep it open through the Eating phase and exit in the Sated period.

- The main advantage of the Gator indicator is the compactness of its display. Instead of drawing three separate SMMAs on the chart, we have all the information provided by them packed into the bars below, which leaves enough space for the application of any number of additional indicators onto the price data.

- The Gator oscillator indicates when the trend is strong or weak but it does not point the direction of the trend. Thus, you should use an extra tool to recognize the trend direction.

Understanding Kaufman's Efficiency Ratio

What is Efficiency Ratio?

- A price move that shows us a trend, also shows us range. When price is trending, and range is high it reflects strong trend and momentum. When price is not moving in a direction, but range is high, the volatility or noise is more

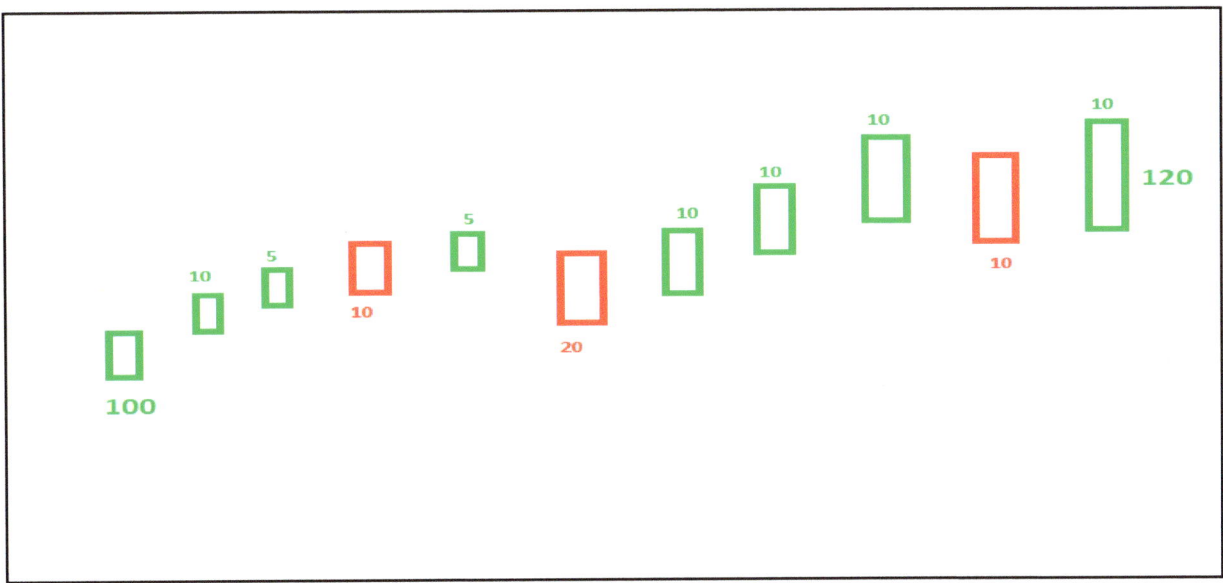

See Above image. It shows daily fluctuation of a stock over 10 sessions. Let us calculate total of daily absolute rate of change (Rate of change (ROC) is a study that measures how much price moved up or down from previous bar. The daily rate of change captures the trend. When we make it absolute, captures volatility):

100 = (10+5+10+5+20+10+10+10+10+10). So, during last 10 sessions, total of daily movement is 100 points. Volatility? Let us call it Noise. Total movement was of 100 points. But over the 10 sessions price went up from 100 to 120.

Rate of change over 10 sessions = 20 points

Total move up and down was 100 points but what was the outcome? Price moved up by 20 points. This is known as **Efficiency Ratio**.

Efficiency ratio (ER) = Trend / Noise

ER in above example is 0.20. It took move of 100 points to gain 20 points.

If price is rising & ER is rising = strong uptrend

If price is falling & ER is rising = strong downtrend

This means there is more of a trend in daily fluctuation.

If ER is falling, noise is more. This way, Efficiency ratio becomes a good volatility indicator.

We can plot the ER indicator on the chart. ER trading above 0.25 (25%) indicates strong trend, it shows strong momentum when it is above 0.40 (40%).

- ER > 0.25 = Strong trend
- ER > 0.40 = Very strong trend
- ER < 0.10 = Dull phase
- ER < 0.05 = Trend might emerge (Volatility cycle)

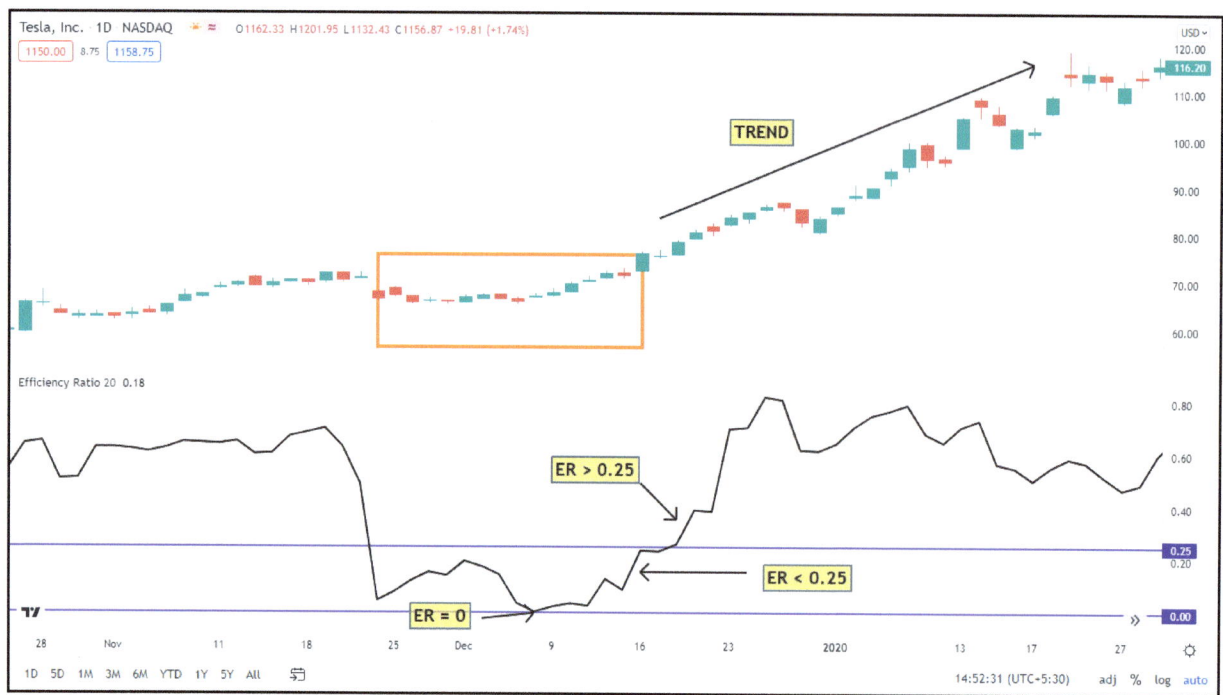

Figure 5: Tesla Inc. Daily Chart

We can plot moving average on chart for trend identification along with ER. Moving average is a trend following indicator. Price crossing moving average is bullish and falling below moving average is bearish. But during sideways or volatile period, price fluctuates around moving average resulting in whipsaws.

To understand better how Efficiency Ratio works, let's take a look at the chart below where you may see 20-day price trends

Figure 5: ITC Ltd. Daily Chart

Application:

- Efficiency Ratio can be used for identifying bullish moves in instances where price had already gone up steeply, but rests. If speculating that price will continually rise, then can enter during resting phase.

- Efficiency Ratio can be used to filter out choppy entry signals produced by existing trade strategies. If trying to enter during periods of consolidation, then ER should ideally be low

- Using the efficiency ratio, you may determine how effective pricing adjustments occur. It moves between 1 and 0 on a scale. ER equals zero (zero) when the price stays constant over a period of ten periods. In contrast, if a price increases or moves down for 10 consecutive periods, the ER is reduced to one. (Note: We can substitute 10 period efficiency ratio to higher/lower period as per our trading strategy)

Figure 6: TATA Chemicals Ltd. Daily Chart, Price and 5 period Moving Average (MA) breakout, signals a change in trend.

Price above 5 period MA	Bullish	Trend>Volatility	5 period MA is rising relatively faster
Price above 5 period MA	Bullish	Trend<Volatility	5 period MA is rising relatively slower
Price below 5 period MA	Bearish	Trend>Volatility	5 period MA is falling relatively faster
Price below 5 period MA	Bearish	Trend<Volatility	5 period MA is falling relatively slower

Conclusion

The Kaufman Efficiency Ratio tries to identify as strong a trend as possible. Positions are taken in the direction of the trend. By doing this Kaufman follows the age old trader saying "the trend is your friend". The Kaufman Efficiency Ratio can be used both for day trading and swing trading. Traders do well to take a look at this indicator as the trend is a key parameter in trading.

Trade Setup: Buy Conditions

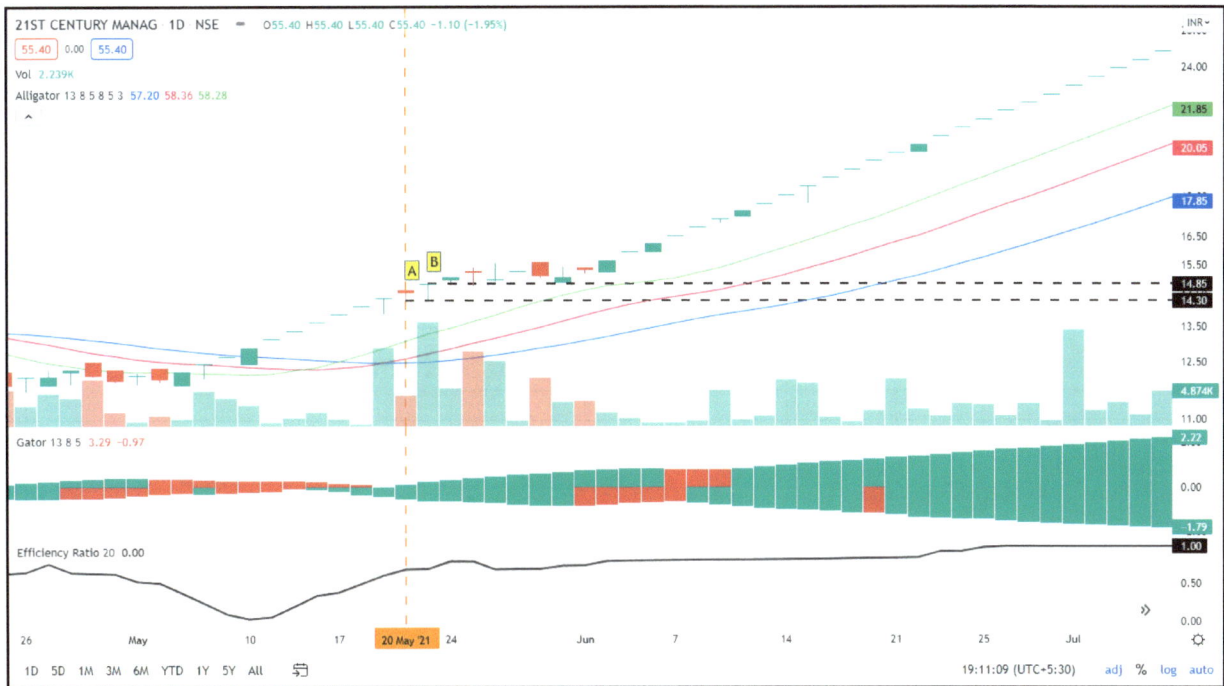

FIGURE 7: 21ˢᵀ CENTURY MANAGEMENT LTD. DAILY CHART

From the above chart, you can see two candles marked as A and B on the Daily Chart. **Candle A** (referred to as the **Signal Candle**) on **May 20, 2021**, is a bullish green candle with a higher high and a higher low. Candle B (referred to as the **Breakout Candle**) on **May 21, 2021**, is also a bullish green candle, which should close above the **high** of the Signal Candle (Candle A). A buy trade should be placed above the high of the Breakout Candle. There are **four conditions** to be met for a potential buy on a positional basis. Here's an interpretation of each condition:

Condition 1: Alligator Indicator

- The Alligator Indicator is best used on the daily time frame.

- A long position can be created when the green line (lip) crosses above the red line (teeth) and the blue line (jaw), with the teeth (red line) above the jaw (blue line).

- The long position can be closed when the green line (lip) moves down and crosses below the red and blue lines (teeth and jaw).

Condition 2: Price & Volume Breakout

- After satisfying the first condition, look for the first candle that forms either a higher high and higher low or an Outside Bar Candle. This will be considered the **Signal Candle** (Candle A). The Signal Candle must close above the **5-period Moving Average** (the green line or lip).

- The second candle should close above the **high** of the **Signal Candle** (Candle A) and will be considered the Breakout Candle (Candle B).

- The volume of the Breakout Candle must be **greater than** that of the Signal Candle.

Condition 3: Gator Oscillator

- For both the Signal Candle (Candle A) and the Breakout Candle (Candle B), the **Gator Oscillator histogram** should not be in a **Sleeping Phase** (i.e., the bars on both sides should not be red).

- The **upper Gator histogram bar** of the Breakout Candle (Candle B) should be **green** and greater in absolute value than that of the Signal Candle (Candle A).

Condition 4: Efficiency Ratio (ER)

- The Efficiency Ratio (ER) of the Breakout Candle (Candle B) should be **greater** than **0.25**.

- The Efficiency Ratio (ER) of the Breakout Candle (Candle B) should also be greater than that of the Signal Candle (Candle A).

- Note: A **15-period Efficiency Ratio** (ER) is used for this trading setup.

- ➢ Once all the above conditions are met, initiate a **buy trade** above the high of the Breakout Candle (Candle B).

- ➢ **Stop Loss Placement**:

    A) Place the stop loss below the low of the Signal Candle (Candle A), or

    B) Below the lowest point of any resting candles between the Signal Candle and Breakout Candle.

    Use whichever value is **higher**.

- ➢ **Target**: Aim for a risk-to-reward ratio of 1:2.

Analysis

INDIAN STOCKS

GOKALDAS EXPORTS	MASTEK
GRAVITA INDIA	NITIN SPINNERS
INDO COUNT INDUSTRIES	PERSISTENT SYSTEMS
JINDAL STAINLESS HISAR	PITTI ENGINEERING
JSW STEEL	PRINCE PIPES FITTINGS
LYKA LABS	RSWM
MARAL OVERSEAS	STEEL AUTHORITY OF INDIA

1. GOKALDAS EXPORTS

FIGURE 8: GOKALDAS EXPORTS Daily Chart

Analysis:

A) On Daily Timeframe, **Alligator Indicator** green line or lip crosses teeth (red line) and jaw (blue line) upwards & teeth (red line) is above jaw (blue line) on **03rd May 2021**
B) Signal Candle made higher high and closed above **5 day period Moving Average** (i.e. green line or lip) on **05th May 2021**
C) Daily Breakout Candle (**06th May 2021**) crossed Signal Candle High (**05th May 2021**) and closed above it
D) Breakout Candle **Volume greater than** Signal Candle **Volume**
E) **Gator Oscillator:**
   - **Gator Oscillator Histogram** is not in a **Sleeping Phase** for both Signal Candle & Breakout Candle
   - **Upper Gator Histogram Bar** of Breakout Candle is **Green Colour** & greater than Signal Candle in absolute number
F) The **Efficiency Ratio (ER)** of Breakout Candle (Candle B) is greater than **0.25**
G) The **Efficiency Ratio (ER)** of Breakout Candle is **greater** Signal Candle

Since all conditions were met, a buy trade would be executed above the high of the Breakout Candle. The stop loss should be placed below the low of the Signal Candle or the lowest Resting Candle between the Signal Candle and Breakout Candle, whichever is higher, with a target set at a 1:2 risk-to-reward ratio.

2. GRAVITA INDIA

FIGURE 9: GRAVITA INDIA Daily Chart

Analysis:

A) On Daily Timeframe, **Alligator Indicator** green line or lip crosses teeth (red line) and jaw (blue line) upwards & teeth (red line) is above jaw (blue line) on **11th June 2021**
B) Signal Candle made higher high and closed above **5 day period Moving Average** (i.e. green line or lip) on **11th June 2021**
C) Daily Breakout Candle (**14th June 2021**) crossed Signal Candle High (**11th June 2021**) and closed above it
D) Breakout Candle **Volume greater than** Signal Candle **Volume**
E) **Gator Oscillator:**
   - **Gator Oscillator Histogram** is not in a **Sleeping Phase** for both Signal Candle & Breakout Candle
   - **Upper Gator Histogram Bar** of Breakout Candle is **Green Colour** & greater than Signal Candle in absolute number
F) The **Efficiency Ratio (ER)** of Breakout Candle (Candle B) is greater than **0.25**
G) The **Efficiency Ratio (ER)** of Breakout Candle is **greater** Signal Candle

Since all conditions were met, a buy trade would be executed above the high of the Breakout Candle. The stop loss should be placed below the low of the Signal Candle or the lowest Resting Candle between the Signal Candle and Breakout Candle, whichever is higher, with a target set at a 1:2 risk-to-reward ratio.

3. INDO COUNT INDUSTRIES

FIGURE 10: INDO COUNT INDUSTRIES Daily Chart

Analysis:

A) On Daily Timeframe, **Alligator Indicator** green line or lip crosses teeth (red line) and jaw (blue line) upwards & teeth (red line) is above jaw (blue line) on **04th May 2021**
B) Signal Candle made higher high and closed above **5 day period Moving Average** (i.e. green line or lip) on **04th May 2021**
C) Daily Breakout Candle (**10th May 2021**) crossed Signal Candle High (**04th May 2021**) and closed above it
D) Breakout Candle **Volume greater than** Signal Candle **Volume**
E) **Gator Oscillator:**
    - **Gator Oscillator Histogram** is not in a **Sleeping Phase** for both Signal Candle & Breakout Candle
    - **Upper Gator Histogram Bar** of Breakout Candle is **Green Colour** & greater than Signal Candle in absolute number
F) The **Efficiency Ratio (ER)** of Breakout Candle (Candle B) is greater than **0.25**
G) The **Efficiency Ratio (ER)** of Breakout Candle is **greater** Signal Candle

Since all conditions were met, a buy trade would be executed above the high of the Breakout Candle. The stop loss should be placed below the low of the Signal Candle or the lowest Resting Candle between the Signal Candle and Breakout Candle, whichever is higher, with a target set at a 1:2 risk-to-reward ratio.

4. JINDAL STAINLESS HISAR

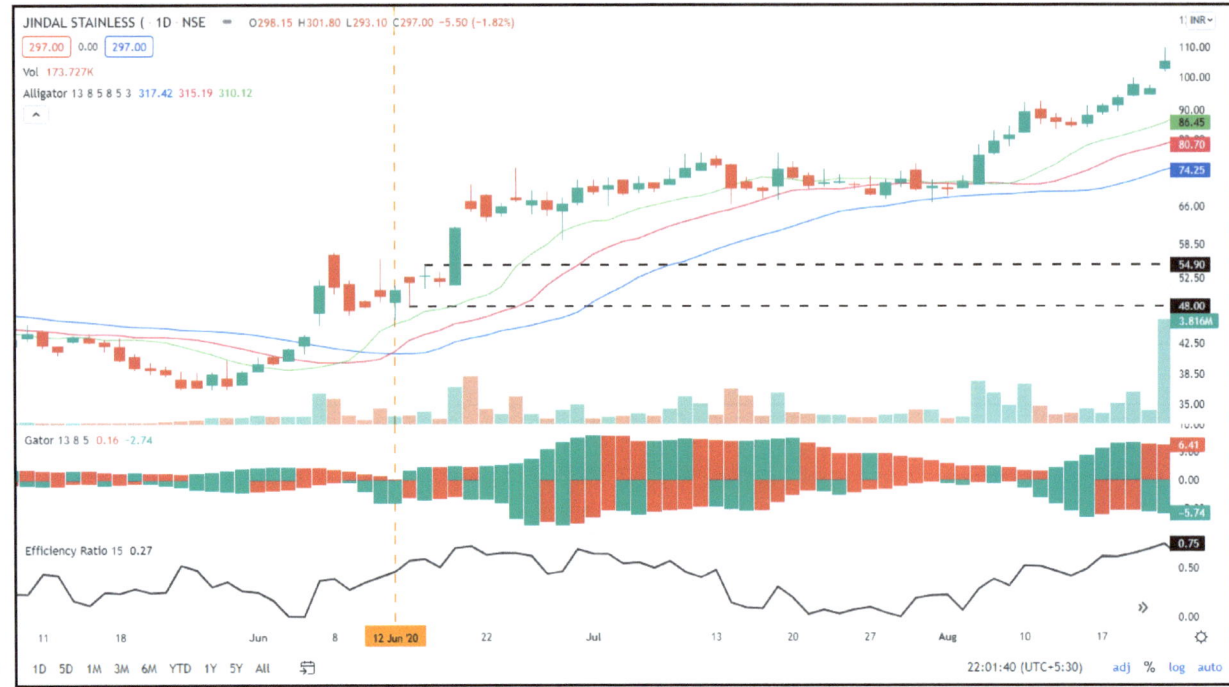

FIGURE 11: JINDAL STAINLESS HISAR Daily Chart

Analysis:

A) On Daily Timeframe, **Alligator Indicator** green line or lip crosses teeth (red line) and jaw (blue line) upwards & teeth (red line) is above jaw (blue line) on **12th June 2020**
B) Signal Candle made higher high and closed above **5 day period Moving Average** (i.e. green line or lip) on **15th June 2020**
C) Daily Breakout Candle (**16th June 2020**) crossed Signal Candle High (**15th June 2020**) and closed above it
D) Breakout Candle **Volume greater than** Signal Candle **Volume**
E) **Gator Oscillator:**
   - **Gator Oscillator Histogram** is not in a **Sleeping Phase** for both Signal Candle & Breakout Candle
   - **Upper Gator Histogram Bar** of Breakout Candle is **Green Colour** & greater than Signal Candle in absolute number
F) The **Efficiency Ratio (ER)** of Breakout Candle (Candle B) is greater than **0.25**
G) The **Efficiency Ratio (ER)** of Breakout Candle is **greater** Signal Candle

Since all conditions were met, a buy trade would be executed above the high of the Breakout Candle. The stop loss should be placed below the low of the Signal Candle or the lowest Resting Candle between the Signal Candle and Breakout Candle, whichever is higher, with a target set at a 1:2 risk-to-reward ratio.

5. JSW STEEL

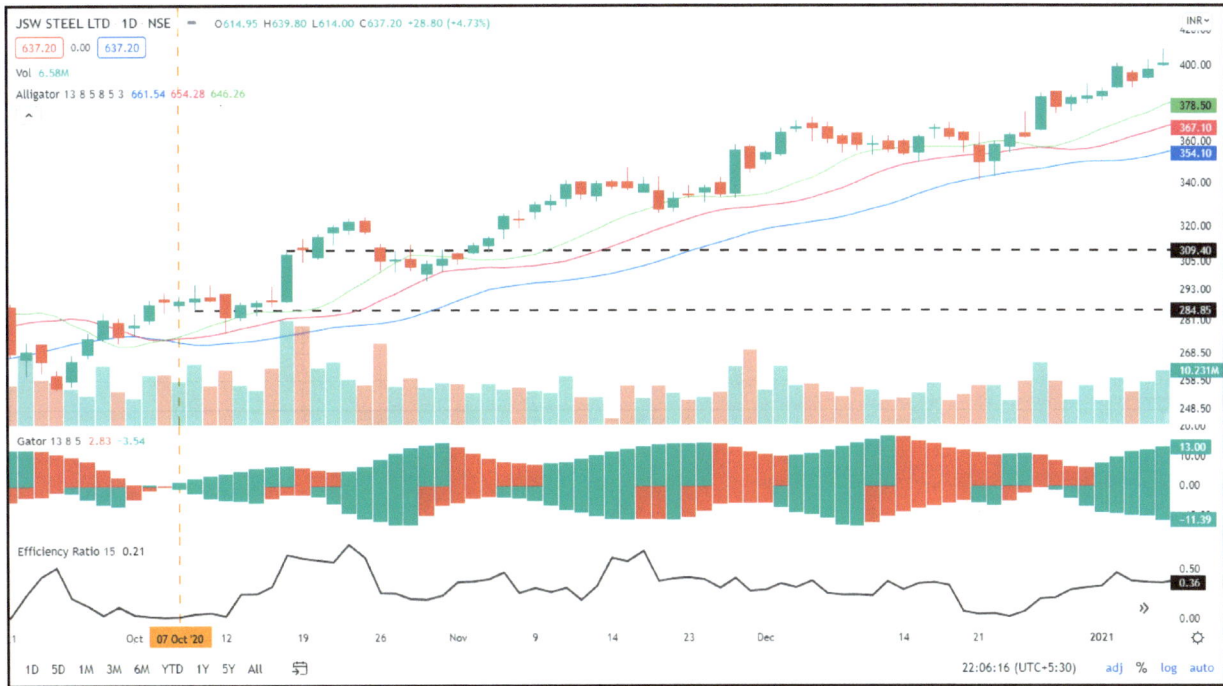

FIGURE 12: JSW STEEL Daily Chart

Analysis:

A) On Daily Timeframe, **Alligator Indicator** green line or lip crosses teeth (red line) and jaw (blue line) upwards & teeth (red line) is above jaw (blue line) on **07th October 2020**
B) Signal Candle made higher high and closed above **5 day period Moving Average** (i.e. green line or lip) on **08th October 2020**
C) Daily Breakout Candle (**16th October 2020**) crossed Signal Candle High (**08th October 2020**) and closed above it
D) Breakout Candle **Volume greater than** Signal Candle **Volume**
E) **Gator Oscillator:**
   - **Gator Oscillator Histogram** is not in a **Sleeping Phase** for both Signal Candle & Breakout Candle
   - **Upper Gator Histogram Bar** of Breakout Candle is **Green Colour** & greater than Signal Candle in absolute number
F) The **Efficiency Ratio (ER)** of Breakout Candle (Candle B) is greater than **0.25**
G) The **Efficiency Ratio (ER)** of Breakout Candle is **greater** Signal Candle

Since all conditions were met, a buy trade would be executed above the high of the Breakout Candle. The stop loss should be placed below the low of the Signal Candle or the lowest Resting Candle between the Signal Candle and Breakout Candle, whichever is higher, with a target set at a 1:2 risk-to-reward ratio.

6. LYKA LABS

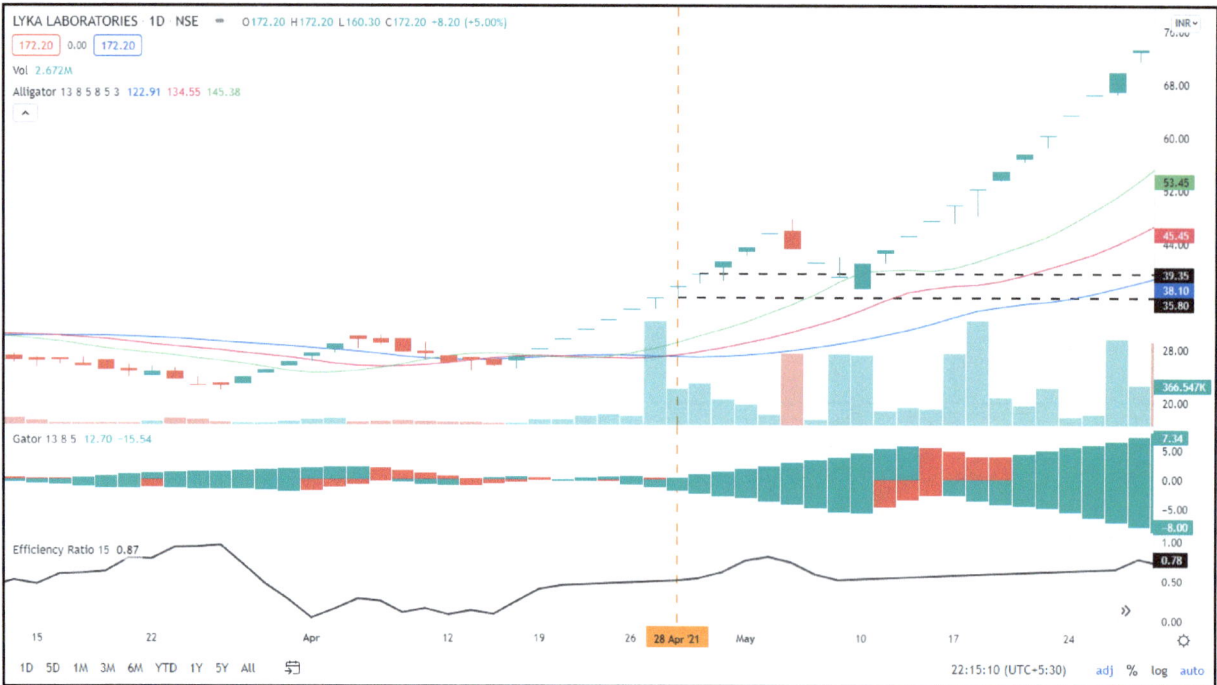

FIGURE 13: LYKA LABS Daily Chart

Analysis:

A) On Daily Timeframe, **Alligator Indicator** green line or lip crosses teeth (red line) and jaw (blue line) upwards & teeth (red line) is above jaw (blue line) on **28th April 2021**
B) Signal Candle made higher high and closed above **5 day period Moving Average** (i.e. green line or lip) on **28th April 2021**
C) Daily Breakout Candle (**29th April 2021**) crossed Signal Candle High (**28th April 2021**) and closed above it
D) Breakout Candle **Volume greater than** Signal Candle **Volume**
E) **Gator Oscillator:**
    - **Gator Oscillator Histogram** is not in a **Sleeping Phase** for both Signal Candle & Breakout Candle
    - **Upper Gator Histogram Bar** of Breakout Candle is **Green Colour** & greater than Signal Candle in absolute number
F) The **Efficiency Ratio (ER)** of Breakout Candle (Candle B) is greater than **0.25**
G) The **Efficiency Ratio (ER)** of Breakout Candle is **greater** Signal Candle

Since all conditions were met, a buy trade would be executed above the high of the Breakout Candle. The stop loss should be placed below the low of the Signal Candle or the lowest Resting Candle between the Signal Candle and Breakout Candle, whichever is higher, with a target set at a 1:2 risk-to-reward ratio.

7. MARAL OVERSEAS

FIGURE 14: MARAL OVERSEAS Daily Chart

Analysis:

A) On Daily Timeframe, **Alligator Indicator** green line or lip crosses teeth (red line) and jaw (blue line) upwards & teeth (red line) is above jaw (blue line) on **03rd May 2021**
B) Signal Candle made higher high and closed above **5 day period Moving Average** (i.e. green line or lip) on **06th May 2021**
C) Daily Breakout Candle (**07th May 2021**) crossed Signal Candle High (**06th May 2021**) and closed above it
D) Breakout Candle **Volume greater than** Signal Candle **Volume**
E) **Gator Oscillator:**
    - **Gator Oscillator Histogram** is not in a **Sleeping Phase** for both Signal Candle & Breakout Candle
    - **Upper Gator Histogram Bar** of Breakout Candle is **Green Colour** & greater than Signal Candle in absolute number
F) The **Efficiency Ratio (ER)** of Breakout Candle (Candle B) is greater than **0.25**
G) The **Efficiency Ratio (ER)** of Breakout Candle is **greater** Signal Candle

Since all conditions were met, a buy trade would be executed above the high of the Breakout Candle. The stop loss should be placed below the low of the Signal Candle or the lowest Resting Candle between the Signal Candle and Breakout Candle, whichever is higher, with a target set at a 1:2 risk-to-reward ratio.

8. MASTEK

FIGURE 15: MASTEK Daily Chart

Analysis:

A) On Daily Timeframe, **Alligator Indicator** green line or lip crosses teeth (red line) and jaw (blue line) upwards & teeth (red line) is above jaw (blue line) on **08th June 2020**
B) Signal Candle made higher high and closed above **5 day period Moving Average** (i.e. green line or lip) on **11th June 2020**
C) Daily Breakout Candle (**15th June 2020**) crossed Signal Candle High (**11th June 2020**) and closed above it
D) Breakout Candle **Volume greater than** Signal Candle **Volume**
E) **Gator Oscillator:**
   - **Gator Oscillator Histogram** is not in a **Sleeping Phase** for both Signal Candle & Breakout Candle
   - **Upper Gator Histogram Bar** of Breakout Candle is **Green Colour** & greater than Signal Candle in absolute number
F) The **Efficiency Ratio (ER)** of Breakout Candle (Candle B) is greater than **0.25**
G) The **Efficiency Ratio (ER)** of Breakout Candle is **greater** Signal Candle

Since all conditions were met, a buy trade would be executed above the high of the Breakout Candle. The stop loss should be placed below the low of the Signal Candle or the lowest Resting Candle between the Signal Candle and Breakout Candle, whichever is higher, with a target set at a 1:2 risk-to-reward ratio.

9. NITIN SPINNERS

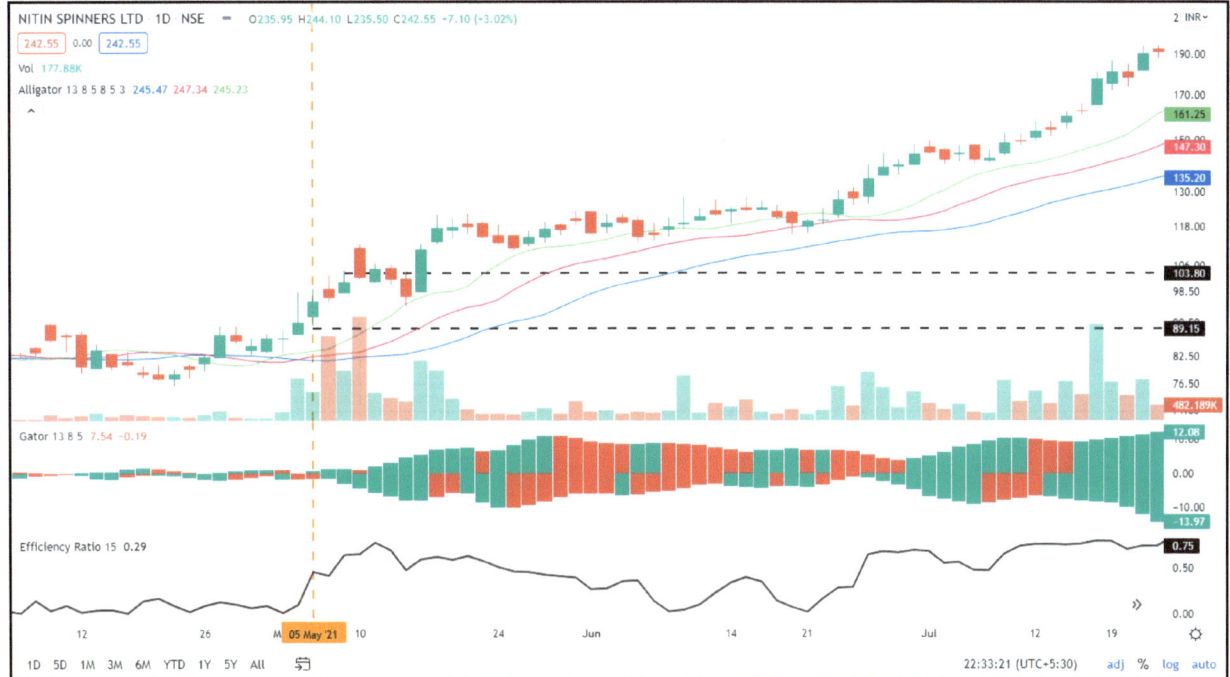

FIGURE 16: NITIN SPINNERS Daily Chart

Analysis:

A) On Daily Timeframe, **Alligator Indicator** green line or lip crosses teeth (red line) and jaw (blue line) upwards & teeth (red line) is above jaw (blue line) on **05th May 2021**
B) Signal Candle made higher high and closed above **5 day period Moving Average** (i.e. green line or lip) on **05th May 2021**
C) Daily Breakout Candle (**07th May 2021**) crossed Signal Candle High (**05th May 2021**) and closed above it
D) Breakout Candle **Volume greater than** Signal Candle **Volume**
E) **Gator Oscillator:**
   - **Gator Oscillator Histogram** is not in a **Sleeping Phase** for both Signal Candle & Breakout Candle
   - **Upper Gator Histogram Bar** of Breakout Candle is **Green Colour** & greater than Signal Candle in absolute number
F) The **Efficiency Ratio (ER)** of Breakout Candle (Candle B) is greater than **0.25**
G) The **Efficiency Ratio (ER)** of Breakout Candle is **greater** Signal Candle

Since all conditions were met, a buy trade would be executed above the high of the Breakout Candle. The stop loss should be placed below the low of the Signal Candle or the lowest Resting Candle between the Signal Candle and Breakout Candle, whichever is higher, with a target set at a 1:2 risk-to-reward ratio.

10. PERSISTENT SYSTEMS

FIGURE 17: PERSISTENT SYSTEMS Daily Chart

Analysis:

A) On Daily Timeframe, **Alligator Indicator** green line or lip crosses teeth (red line) and jaw (blue line) upwards & teeth (red line) is above jaw (blue line) on **03rd December 2020**
B) Signal Candle made higher high and closed above **5 day period Moving Average** (i.e. green line or lip) on **03rd December 2020**
C) Daily Breakout Candle (**11th December 2020**) crossed Signal Candle High (**03rd December 2020**) and closed above it
D) Breakout Candle **Volume greater than** Signal Candle **Volume**
E) **Gator Oscillator:**
   - **Gator Oscillator Histogram** is not in a **Sleeping Phase** for both Signal Candle & Breakout Candle
   - **Upper Gator Histogram Bar** of Breakout Candle is **Green Colour** & greater than Signal Candle in absolute number
F) The **Efficiency Ratio (ER)** of Breakout Candle (Candle B) is greater than **0.25**
G) The **Efficiency Ratio (ER)** of Breakout Candle is **greater** Signal Candle

Since all conditions were met, a buy trade would be executed above the high of the Breakout Candle. The stop loss should be placed below the low of the Signal Candle or the lowest Resting Candle between the Signal Candle and Breakout Candle, whichever is higher, with a target set at a 1:2 risk-to-reward ratio.

11. PITTI ENGINEERING

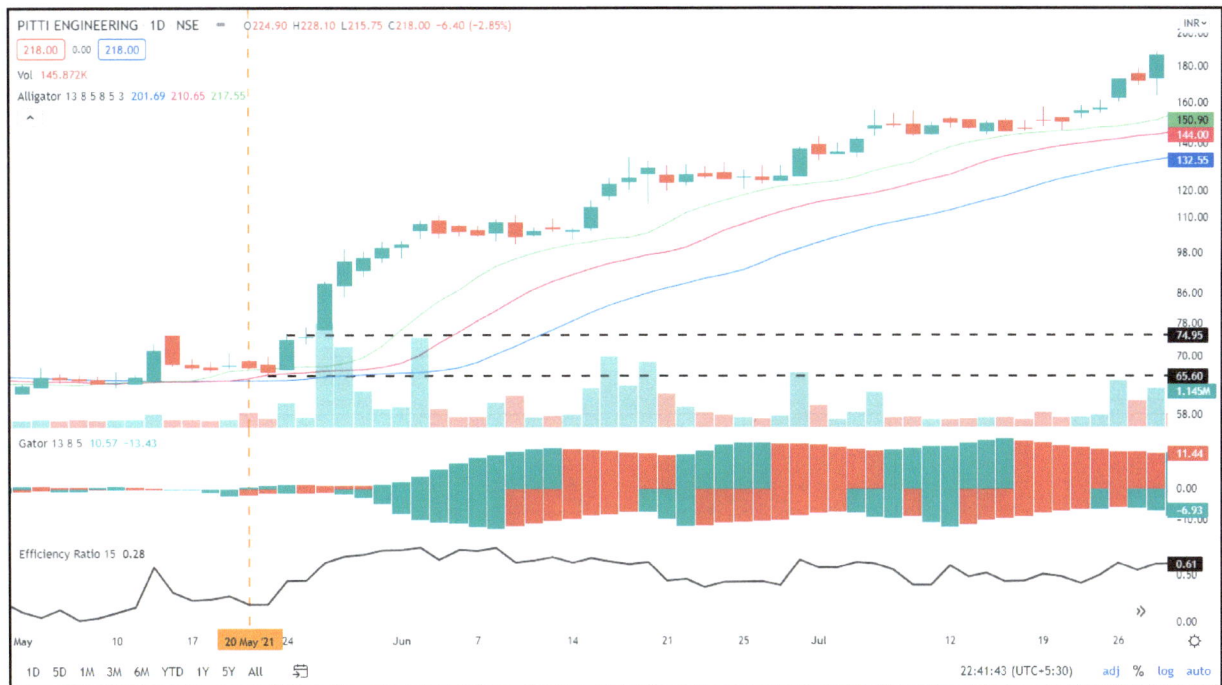

FIGURE 18: PITTI ENGINEERING Daily Chart

Analysis:

A) On Daily Timeframe, **Alligator Indicator** green line or lip crosses teeth (red line) and jaw (blue line) upwards & teeth (red line) is above jaw (blue line) on **20th May 2021**
B) Signal Candle made higher high and closed above **5 day period Moving Average** (i.e. green line or lip) on **21st May 2021**
C) Daily Breakout Candle (**24th May 2021**) crossed Signal Candle High (**21st May 2021**) and closed above it
D) Breakout Candle **Volume greater than** Signal Candle **Volume**
E) **Gator Oscillator:**
   - **Gator Oscillator Histogram** is not in a **Sleeping Phase** for both Signal Candle & Breakout Candle
   - **Upper Gator Histogram Bar** of Breakout Candle is **Green Colour** & greater than Signal Candle in absolute number
F) The **Efficiency Ratio (ER)** of Breakout Candle (Candle B) is greater than **0.25**
G) The **Efficiency Ratio (ER)** of Breakout Candle is **greater** Signal Candle

Since all conditions were met, a buy trade would be executed above the high of the Breakout Candle. The stop loss should be placed below the low of the Signal Candle or the lowest Resting Candle between the Signal Candle and Breakout Candle, whichever is higher, with a target set at a 1:2 risk-to-reward ratio.

12. PRINCE PIPES FITTINGS

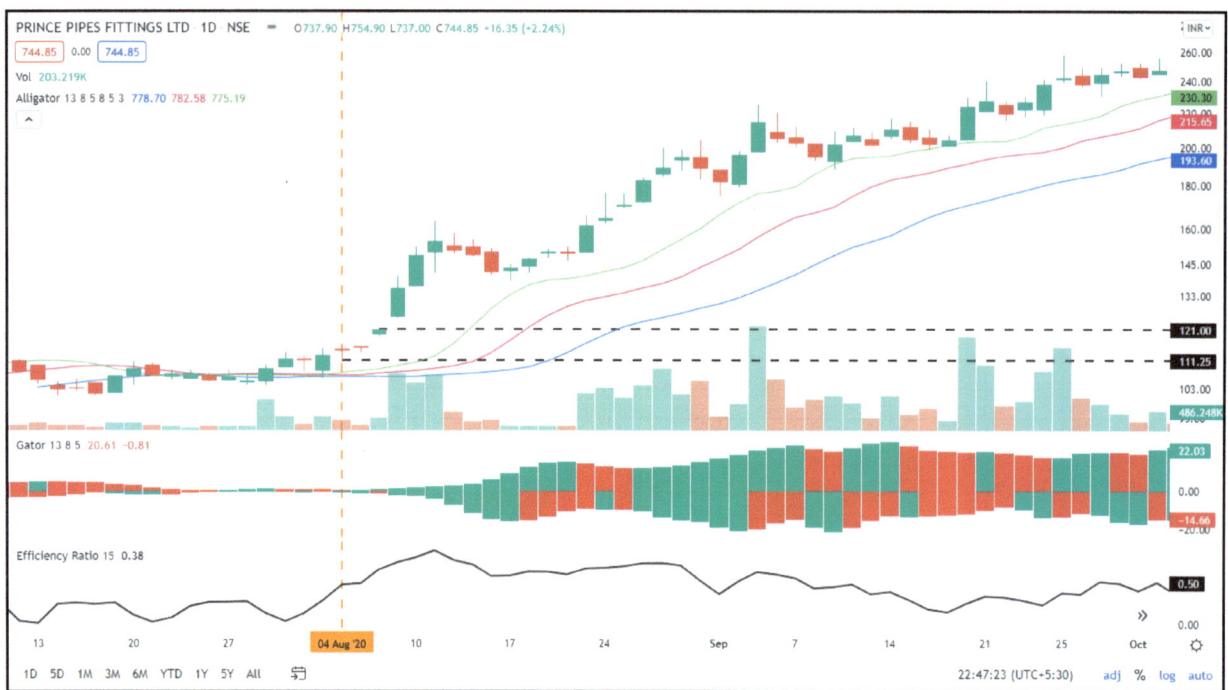

FIGURE 19: PRINCE PIPES FITTINGS Daily Chart

Analysis:

A) On Daily Timeframe, **Alligator Indicator** green line or lip crosses teeth (red line) and jaw (blue line) upwards & teeth (red line) is above jaw (blue line) on **04th August 2020**
B) Signal Candle made higher high and closed above **5 day period Moving Average** (i.e. green line or lip) on **04th August 2020**
C) Daily Breakout Candle (**06th August 2020**) crossed Signal Candle High (**04th August 2020**) and closed above it
D) Breakout Candle **Volume greater than** Signal Candle **Volume**
E) **Gator Oscillator:**
   - **Gator Oscillator Histogram** is not in a **Sleeping Phase** for both Signal Candle & Breakout Candle
   - **Upper Gator Histogram Bar** of Breakout Candle is **Green Colour** & greater than Signal Candle in absolute number
F) The **Efficiency Ratio (ER)** of Breakout Candle (Candle B) is greater than **0.25**
G) The **Efficiency Ratio (ER)** of Breakout Candle is **greater** Signal Candle

Since all conditions were met, a buy trade would be executed above the high of the Breakout Candle. The stop loss should be placed below the low of the Signal Candle or the lowest Resting Candle between the Signal Candle and Breakout Candle, whichever is higher, with a target set at a 1:2 risk-to-reward ratio.

13. RSWM

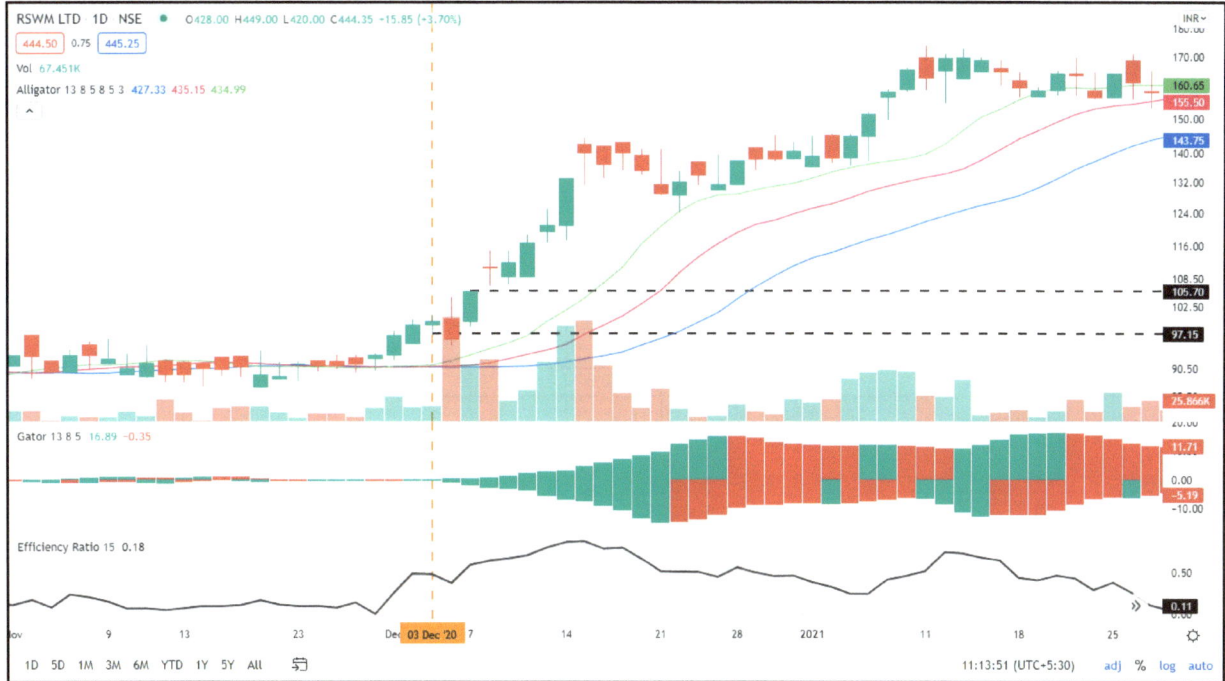

FIGURE 20: RSWM Daily Chart

Analysis:

A) On Daily Timeframe, **Alligator Indicator** green line or lip crosses teeth (red line) and jaw (blue line) upwards & teeth (red line) is above jaw (blue line) on **03rd December 2020**
B) Signal Candle made higher high and closed above **5 day period Moving Average** (i.e. green line or lip) on **03rd December 2020**
C) Daily Breakout Candle (**07th December 2020**) crossed Signal Candle High (**03rd December 2020**) and closed above it
D) Breakout Candle **Volume greater than** Signal Candle **Volume**
E) **Gator Oscillator:**
   - **Gator Oscillator Histogram** is not in a **Sleeping Phase** for both Signal Candle & Breakout Candle
   - **Upper Gator Histogram Bar** of Breakout Candle is **Green Colour** & greater than Signal Candle in absolute number
F) The **Efficiency Ratio (ER)** of Breakout Candle (Candle B) is greater than **0.25**
G) The **Efficiency Ratio (ER)** of Breakout Candle is **greater** Signal Candle

Since all conditions were met, a buy trade would be executed above the high of the Breakout Candle. The stop loss should be placed below the low of the Signal Candle or the lowest Resting Candle between the Signal Candle and Breakout Candle, whichever is higher, with a target set at a 1:2 risk-to-reward ratio.

14. STEEL AUTHORITY OF INDIA

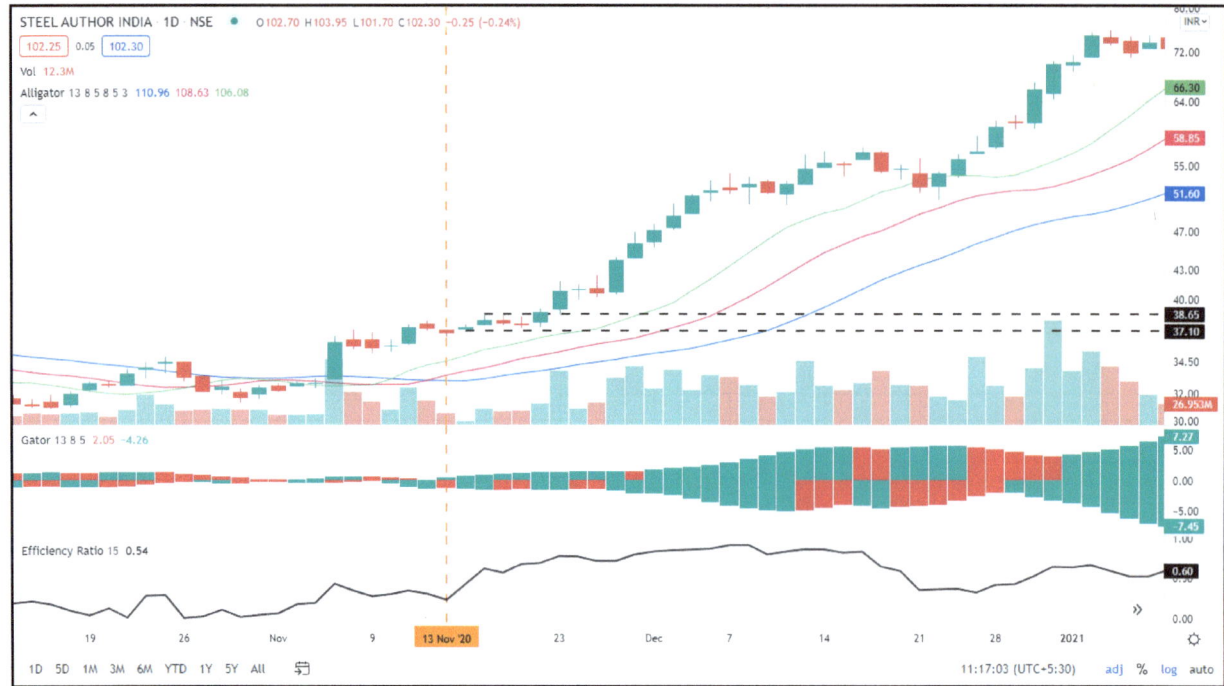

FIGURE 21: STEEL AUTHORITY OF INDIA Daily Chart

Analysis:

A) On Daily Timeframe, **Alligator Indicator** green line or lip crosses teeth (red line) and jaw (blue line) upwards & teeth (red line) is above jaw (blue line) on **13th November 2020**
B) Signal Candle made higher high and closed above **5 day period Moving Average** (i.e. green line or lip) on **14th November 2020**
C) Daily Breakout Candle (**17th November 2020**) crossed Signal Candle High (**14th November 2020**) and closed above it
D) Breakout Candle **Volume greater than** Signal Candle **Volume**
E) **Gator Oscillator:**
   - **Gator Oscillator Histogram** is not in a **Sleeping Phase** for both Signal Candle & Breakout Candle
   - **Upper Gator Histogram Bar** of Breakout Candle is **Green Colour** & greater than Signal Candle in absolute number
F) The **Efficiency Ratio (ER)** of Breakout Candle (Candle B) is greater than **0.25**
G) The **Efficiency Ratio (ER)** of Breakout Candle is **greater** Signal Candle

Since all conditions were met, a buy trade would be executed above the high of the Breakout Candle. The stop loss should be placed below the low of the Signal Candle or the lowest Resting Candle between the Signal Candle and Breakout Candle, whichever is higher, with a target set at a 1:2 risk-to-reward ratio.

Summary

The Alligator Indicator is a trend-following tool designed to help traders identify trending markets. The Gator Oscillator, also developed by Bill Williams, complements the Alligator Indicator by highlighting the strength of trends and ranges using a histogram rather than moving averages. Both indicators excel in markets exhibiting strong directional momentum.

Kaufman's Efficiency Ratio, developed by Perry Kaufman, is commonly used by traders as a filter to avoid trading in "choppy" or sideways markets. It helps to distinguish between volatile price movements and smoother, more predictable trends, improving trade selection.

Mastering Breakout Trading: A Step-by-Step Guide Using the Alligator, Gator Oscillator & Efficiency Ratio is a swing trading strategy that aims to capture substantial gains. This simple yet effective strategy allows traders to enter positions in the direction of the prevailing trend with a tighter stop loss, thanks to favourable trade locations, resulting in a superior risk-to-reward ratio. With proper execution, this strategy can deliver highly accurate and profitable trades.

For any additional details or clarifications, feel free to reach out to me at **wisdomtranquil@gmail.com**. I would be more than happy to assist you in further understanding this strategy with my humble insights.